Hawk's Cry

poems by

Mary Pacifico Curtis

Finishing Line Press
Georgetown, Kentucky

Hawk's Cry

Copyright © 2023 by Mary Pacifico Curtis
ISBN 979-8-88838-141-0 First Edition
All rights reserved under International and Pan-American Copyright Conventions. No part of this book may be reproduced in any manner whatsoever without written permission from the publisher, except in the case of brief quotations embodied in critical articles and reviews.

ACKNOWLEDGMENTS

The following poems appeared or are forthcoming as noted, some in earlier versions.

Clutching at Straws: "Haiti, 2010"
Los Positas Literary Review: "Stonehenge" and "The Face of the Moon"
Boston Literary Magazine: "A Wife Contemplates the Pulley" and "Convertible"
Tiferet Journal Poetry Contest 2019 Finalist: "Ubi Caritas"
Narrative Magazine: "Shepherd, Shepherd Where Are You?"
Catamaran: "Ghost Tree"
Naugatuck River Review Poetry Contest 2020 Finalist: "Of Men Who Stayed"
The Fourth River: "Silent No More"
Synkroniciti: "The Hawk Circles," "Hello Grief, Garden, Hawk;" "The Shepherd's Refrain," and "Seeker's Poem"
Sixfold: "Day of the Deer," "White Wings," and "Ubi Caritas"
Milagros Anthology (Bourne Poetry): "Quaero"

With gratitude to Tupelo Press for The 30/30 Project, where several of the poems in this collection were born.

Publisher: Leah Huete de Maines
Editor: Christen Kincaid
Cover Art: Kathryn Dunlevie
Author Photo: Laura Turbow Photography
Cover Design: Elizabeth Maines McCleavy

Order online: www.finishinglinepress.com
also available on amazon.com

Author inquiries and mail orders:
Finishing Line Press
P. O. Box 1626
Georgetown, Kentucky 40324
U. S. A.

Table of Contents

The hawk circles

I

One by One 1
Haiti, 2010 2
The World Still Waits 3
Being. A Father 4
A Wife Contemplates the Pulley 6
On Death Row 7
5 Stories Above 9
Of Men Who Stayed... 10
Silent No More.. 12
Meditation on Kintsukuroi 14
The Gift 15
White Wings 16
Ubi cáritas est vera, est vera. Deus ibi est. 17
Shepherd, Shepherd, Where Are You?................................... 18
Hunger 20
Burning 21
Uroborous.. 22
The Scream 23
Imperfect Perfect 24
The Shepherd's Refrain: It Is Coming 25

Canary in rare olive

II

The Baritone in St. Barts... 31
Grace Notes... 33
Home.. 35
Four Chambers Redacted.. 37
Convertible.. 39

Behind the Moon 40
The Face of the Moon 42
Landing 43
A Child Of The Fifties Looks Out On A Lake 44
Just Kids Again 45
Horsemen of Earlier Years 46

You cry out

III

Seeker's Poem 51
Ghost Tree 53
Stonehenge 54
Day of the Deer 56
Wrong Turn 57
Curator 58
Seen in Stone 59
You Rode Your Horses 60
Slightly 62
Orb 64
Photographer's Proclamation 65
Quaero 66
Hello Grief, Garden, Hawk 67
Another Moment in the Garden of Eden 68

Notes 69

The hawk circles

*on the ground
our transgressions
on pause*

*his arc and swerve
red tail spread
white chest*

*black wings
reach wide
his head*

fixed

*he stirs
the skies
one circle*

*and then
another.*

I

One by One

Among the wooden pews and rows
of supplicants in separate reverie,

the one who feels age take hold
lifts chin and eyes
to the crucifix, the life-sized
man whose ribs
can be counted, one
by one,

his clavicle a hollow,
his adam's apple a stone,

his eyes alive
with gentler doctrine
than the preaching
of predestined hell.

His stretched arms embrace death
slender, sinewed, smelling
of grit
sweat
sun and dust.
His cry forever living

before the pressed, pleated
and fine who come here,

each with an ache
comforted in silence,
smooth wood
and the nails that pierced
his limbs.

Haiti, 2010

The girl-child is one
among thousands
—round belly girded
by obvious ribs,
her brown twig arm
with willow digits
outstretched, glittering
brown pools for eyes
holding this moment
and the ones before
amputation and pain
controlled, now with
cookie in hand
she urges her surgeon
to enjoy the sweet.

The World Still Waits

—as Nelson Mandela declined

as he lived   frail   furrowed
flat now between whites

his faint words thunder
through time   continents   clashes
swarms of fists and cries

between life and death.
In white limestone under island sun
he smolders still

giving sustenance
—though a black man's prison meals did not—
fanning imperfect freedom

to flame.

Being. A Father.

They know what we don't know or think about
today I wake up to a steady motorized noise…the water heater…
it is my son, Walker
he may be trying to stimulate himself
operate as others do—do things as others do

He gives his head a little bang
kind of laughs   he can't speak
he's fed through a tube
we spent a long time figuring out how to communicate

he's bald as a space man, very small at 15
looks 10 with the mind of a 2 1/2-year-old
"we do want him to live, don't we?" asked the doctor

Imagine a world with only
masters of the universe—like Sparta.

Walker is a way of being, an alternate way of being
I thought he was a psychopath until I saw
he's smarter, outwits me, you just have be with him

I can fail with him, a mutual admission
neither of you knows what to do

it's harder and way more graceful than anyone imagines

people never know what it's like to live in the body and mind
of a Walker—is there a pleasure in the existence?
there is no evidence that his life is happy
he spends much of his life crying

I think it's agony when he's hitting himself, I don't know what's happening
and there are times he's happy and as happy as you can imagine
somehow his sister and doctor   make him widely joyous

he's in great pain, he has great laughter he bangs his head, he's in a home.
My little boy has gone away? He has a life of his own

they give us more than we will ever give them
they know   about being
they know   things that we forget

A Wife Contemplates The Pulley

—2010, Copiapo, Chile

over the edge of a pit
this hole in the ground stretches
twenty-stories

my husband is down there

his travel supports our family
now engineers have our lives
in their hands

they recommend beams
a structure   pulley   cage

in the beginning
we didn't know if
he could live

then my flimsy faith
and I need to know

if a man would eat someone
if one cried in the headlamp glow
lighting the fallen   if a mistress waits too

if they talk about the jagged rock
edges of starvation
this community of savages hoping

for salvation

I imagine and cannot as that cage drills in
that mere ropes in a shaft can rescue men.

On Death Row

The struggle for justice doesn't end with me
Troy Anthony Davis 1968-2011

I. Cell

I hold him in a stone embrace—he's here to die
like all the rest. My cold heart holds no sentiment
for grizzly souls, bones that settle on my benches
—and, no tenderness for warden, chaplain, deputy.
They all scrape through my arteries—steel bars and
white walled passageways and cells. The Georgia
summers warm this air when sun streams through
the cells' high windows and particles of dust hang,
light in humid glare. The stench those days is sweat
not stuff they use to mask latrines. The ones who
pass this way whisper, sob and kick their innocence,
their protest to my unyielding walls. But this Troy
Davis, he's different in that way. Broadcasts follow
his appeals, his claim he didn't have a gun that night.

II. Lawyer

>He knows we
>are fighting for him
>
>In his heart
>God, let them win
>
>with their words
>and the tv
>
>Words words words
>then silence
>
>appeal denied
>that's it
>
>no chaplain
>no final meal—he fasts.
>
>Just the short walk
>to the room. The gurney.

III. Words

I ask to my family and friends that you all
continue to pray,
that you all continue to forgive.
Continue to fight this fight.

For those about to take my life,
my God have mercy
on all of your souls.

God bless you all,

IV. End

buzz of lights

metal taste
between my tongue and teeth

I lay my body,
rest my head

for the tightening
wrists, ankles, pelvis, chest,

I'm strapped
I breathe

light

faces

the last touch to my earthly skin

the stick

fire

ice.

5 Stories Below

The Styx flows on 5th
where gods and goddesses
lurch and holler for Olympus
(or any other fix).

Artemis stole the tune box—
and she's programming
Chaos in thumping bass,

Oizys shimmies in, snarling,
dissolving like powdered sugar
stirred into liquid misery.

A rare thundercloud
erases the moon
and clears, the LA miracle
that Moros misses. We rise

from our half REM state.
These gods
are not to be ignored.

Along 5th to Grand, released
by Nyx, they sleep by day,
deities in tarps and bags
protecting first-world filth.

Psychopompas guides us.
We pass by Meth,
the new street goddess,
a statue. Just another myth

along the scorched concrete.

Of Men Who Stayed

—Sendai, March 2011

a daughter speaks
through a translator
as blue masks move
through unseeable
particle poison.

*They sleep in shifts
in a room like a living room.*
Video airs
blue, masked men
as in an ether dream.

Lead plated helicopters
drop water from buckets,
land it wide,
a steam plume
that splits blue sky
missing the rods,
a feeble spray.

Unsettled underground
plates push again,
rock hits rock,
teeth grinding against
this cheek of island

where red, black and gold *joro-gumo*
spin their webs outside temples
of gold, black and red,

nishikigoi fatted on algae glint
mottles of orange, white, black
in moats and mortuary ponds—
sentinels of centuries,
entitled species,

geisha walk in town,
tsuma keep the home
bijinesuman drink, fall
into subways, sleep in drawers
in the land of all for one.

Now rock against rock
land of the rising earth, rising wave
rising plume, fallen towns

land of the ones who stayed.

Silent No More

—after the Ai Weiwei installation, Straight

    grey mist over shadow mountains
                landscapes mute in smog
    blur of bicycles   families of three
    140 characters   picture posts
                      unsigned

    then roiling earth hurls rubble
          plaster dust   stucco bits   broken brick
               stone   roof tile shards
        water pooled at pipes   rebar

    scattered bodies
                        the children.

       We must find them.

Excavation, aftershocks and tears
         the waters' soggy churn
              fissures
      on earth's disordered crust

shattered trust
      more silence
    counting

                  but never naming
      the dead.

The children must be named, Fǔbài must be made known.

Mallet and muscle applied to tons
                  uneven rebar pounded straight
—rusted rods

One for every child.

now stacked to model peaks and rolling hills,
                a river gash and sunken plain.

Fluorescents flicker over the ballroom gallery,
         printouts along high walls
streaming names   as living masses

        shudder through in silence,
           circling
the pounded,   sentinel terrain

perfected by excavators
        who reshaped twisted rebar,

into valleys and hillsides, rivers and plains
            unyielding elegy

               to undeniable remains.

Meditation on *Kintsukuroi*

How to seal the ozone hole,
stem snow melt at the poles.
turn back wild winds and fires,
restore species newly gone?

Can a bubble of gold fill fissures we have made?

How to come together when
our backs are up, turned and bent
by the weight of discord we sow,
faction and fracture, a gash
bleeding between us?

Perhaps lacquer-dusted platinum to glue the pieces?

The shattered bowl no longer whole
Irreparable to be thrown away or
do we take the jagged shards to make
—not the thing that was—
but with precious metals as glue,
transformed, to be endowed anew.

The Gift

—James W. Patridge, August 4, 1947-January 23, 2011

He heard   heaved himself into his chair   rolled across the field
to a stand of oaks that blocked his passage   launched onto his chest
creeping through low shrubs   his blind eyes following the cry
to the pool's edge   the toddler   he turned her head   breathed

water rolled   she lived

Flailing arms hadn't kept her afloat   he had no legs
his strength had welled from a frozen moment   Viet Nam
under dull grey   lingering puffs   land mine rubble
a child in tatters   pulled him loose   dragged him

to thicket edging the field.

White Wings

—June 2011, Endeavor's final flight

   The thrust, the dare
to dive and penetrate
a hadal realm of eyes
   that don't know light

   Sticks rubbed together,
ice made into lens,
flint against steel,
   the spark

Endeavour hurtling
above continents
   no longer.
She lumbers,

   a vessel atop a cylinder
crossing borders
invisible
   from the firmament

   white wings under cumuli
clear to cornea upward
   turned

   the steady climb
to cirro clouds,
vaulted into
a God's-eye view.

Ubi cáritas est vera, est vera. Deus ibi est.

—*Easter 2019*

I.
A thick wood ridge runs the length of the sanctuary. Between its downward sloping beams, wood rectangles frame 28 ornamental tiles. Multiply that by seven sections & by two sides of the church. My oldest daughter confessed she calculated the number of ceiling tiles for 8 years during weekly masses. We baptized our girls here, memorialized their dad when he succumbed to cancer. "He didn't want to die," said the priest. ✝ Holy doorways sheltered Joanie who sat upright in her bed of tatters shouting, " Leave me alone, get outta here, fuck you, leave me alone." ✝ The Spanish teacher taught that homosexuality is a sin. Bullying began in the primary grades. Parking lot chatter broke marriages & provoked the occasional restraining order. Moms met up for kickboxing & shared wisdom on sizing implants for perfect tits. "We are the body of Christ. We have to be God's hands, feet, voice." ✝ One Christmas Eve, the priest asked who had come to earth. In an echoing moment of silence, a 3 year-old answered, "Santa Claus!" ✝ Christmas yet again. I snarl under a mask of smiles in the sanctuary. Year after year.

II.
Notre Dame de Paris burned at the beginning of Holy Week.
    Our Lady of Paris.
Mother of continents and genocides.
Mother to immigrant boats tossed in high waves.
Mother church to fathers and mothers
                          torn from little children.

Our Lady's steeple falls.
    Votive memorials persist.
flame against flame.

    Sometimes it causes me to tremble.

Shepherd, Shepherd, Where are You?

—Arab Spring, 2011

I.
It was a season cracked open

II.
flowering honeysuckle
full fragrance of saffron,
mint, and thyme

a season of ripe pomegranates
and aubergines, olives,
and figs on shared borders.

III.
The people awakened, rose up,
raged at tyrants
garbed in uniforms and robes.

Gouty, engorged by their plunder
gated and guarded
they fell,

IV.
awash in their own blood.

V.
It was a time
of blinking characters
on my four walled screens.

Hawks perched, vigilant.
Shepherds slept.

VI.
I cocooned under a black sky.

VII.
We are your sheep,

VIII.
spinning,
choking
in our own dust storms,

IX.
a herd without water
or fruits of the pasture
or peace under the stars.

X.
Shepherd, oh shepherd?

XI.
I awaken, as

XII.
on morning thermals
the red-tailed hawk
lifts,
sounds his cry.

Hunger

The ragged cliff has thousand faces in a thousand hours.
  —*Ralph Waldo Emerson*

It gnaws within the cars filing through, the families they hold.
The trunks opened to accept food.

Hunger is a steep cliff,
hunger is a rainbow

People who clean, hoist, serve unseen,
hospitality at a low wage.

Thank you, *Gracias por todos*. My children thank you,
signs in the dashboards.

It gnaws within the soul. To know
to feel our fortune,

to see the fading of the rainbow
the pilfered pot,

poverty soon amplified by time.
This virus hasn't slowed.

Enough. To know for every face we see
so many more.

Burning

The sky glows orange.
The baby grabs me, grinning.
People talk apocalypse.
In the morning we drive
               as in the night,
headlights on.

We have heard that after
a day of heat snow fell.
               Not here.

The baby tries to make our sounds.
He wants to say our words.
He stands but doesn't notice
               he's not holding on.

The sky is like this now. Some say
it's fire season. Disaster again.
It goes like this, the world is changed.
               Is this new life now,

A world I love, but how?

Uroborous

where house and hearth are out of reach, causing families to flee
        inland to dry fields, orchards and croplands
where immigrants labor in layers of shirts and kerchiefs,
        flimsy filters against round-up,
where black widows, wasps and ticks soak in sun, lurk in shade.

When did I find out that mud and moon and the gaze of a child
        are answers,
that I know earwigs but not *mannu, metope, barro, tin, ni, lotto, tango;*
that poets sing the language of nations,

that salt, life crust, plant slime, debris crackle, and humanity
wash in and out of every sea, greet the tides each day
with cacophony, expectation, net and skiff.

        When did I understand that everything I know is not enough?

The Scream

—after Edvard Munch

Your bruises
brought you
to this moment—

frozen canvas,
silent canvas,
as silent as you are now.

Nighttime by the triple rail—
wide eyes, oval mouth—
a frozen face framed
by orange sea,
singed orb
against
the night,

colors seek their place
in the sea, sky, orb—agitation
of blue, orange, black—
in my heart
against
the night
between us.

Imperfect Perfect

Little twisted girl, oh
        no, that's me

        your hands curl, my heart races
we talk

        you on a screen I struggle to read,
you work so hard to be 'heard.'

I lose interest in being heard, turn
        to the white sun and wonder

        about neurons and electricity,
interior shapes that others cannot see.

        My own genes and cells
formed me with a lesser heart.

You are we, the ones who smile
        and mean it, the ones

        who don't turn away.
You bring us together

in our thriving under
        sunlight and reflection

to live with how we're formed.
        We look into each others' eyes

and become the most perfect
        imperfect sisters.

The Shepherd's Refrain: It Is Coming

—inspired by Greta Thunberg, United Nations, September 24, 2020

The girl perches,
her sight piercing
parched landscapes,
newly shaped shorelines,

fading islands,
ravaging storms,
scorching sun,
crackling nightfall.

It is a time of crossing
spectral bridges,
navigating
through shadows,

A time
when lesser birds fall
from the shroud,
once air.

Hawks cry.

Canary in rare olive,
Throated,
golden trills,

canary in a brass cage.
throw the latch
wide open but

watch—the red-tail hovers.
Soar, child,
into the light.

II

The Baritone in St. Barts

      The man in a fine suit   bella figura

strands imported many inches from one ear
over his shiny pate, illusion of hair,
the suit fitted to his noble stance
without a trace of his Ellis Island passage

      This is the man who enters the sanctuary,

its quiet dark broken
by light filtered through stained
glass clerestory, a diffused scattering
of particles that hang above him
as he walks the naves cold stones
his toes landing at outward angles
to his body, heels hitting loud
his fine suit flexing against his form
in fabric waves.

      The man wraps one hand around

a smaller one, a girl tiny at his side
who wonders what they will do next
and is willing, only still suspecting
as they stroll by empty wooden pews
how wonderful he really is, this father
who is big, smells of his own
generous cologne, and tells her she
is his princess.

      They reach the front, she looks up

at him and he returns her gaze,
a shared surmising,
that she will love him even though—
that he can never be what she calls
him, Daddy. Even then they know

      and look away, both wondering

what they will do next, fragile
in this empty sanctuary, this girl, this man,
and some compulsion to fill the chamber
—disturb and shape the light—
he drops her tiny hand and opens his mouth
wider and wider to the anguish
of his song, theirs,

      what is and will not be.

Grace Notes

Joie de Vivre
        A man met a woman on a business trip.
        No—scratch that.
        They rendezvous'd in Manhattan,
        a bridge away
        from his family home.
        She flirted,
        he strutted designer threads.
        They coupled—and voila!—

        a darling to her father
        twice a year,
        his princess in worsted wool.

City Window
        She takes the frozen milk
        from the window well

        where it is stored in winter—
        with the bread, cottage cheese
        and iced over vegetables—

        sometimes sucking the white ice
        sometimes waiting
        for flavors of the thaw.

Camp
        One summertime
        the girl went to camp
        in a brownstone mansion
        with swings and a slide
        outside   girls
        she didn't know
        weren't kind.
        She ran below
        to the mud-smell basement
        and Clarence the janitor

fat and welcoming   bleach-scented
held her loosely   smiled and put
a pudgy hand   fingers climbing
her tiny leg   reaching firm.
She looked at his roundness
said, *How would you like it if I did that to you*
he said, *Go ahead.*
She ran
but returned.

The Deal

She wished
her father would take her
into the family
he'd made
but
he'd made his deal
sights set.
Cut out the bullshit
he said of poetry
(ironic from a poet).
She gave up poetry,
he died without it.

At twenty-three
she knew
one day
two bucks
would come
and that
would be
his end.

Two greenbacks
hit her mailbox.

Home

Oh, aroma   sizzling onion.

Sundays I cooked in our studio kitchen
  scent of ground beef browning in the pan.

She watched Flipper when I finally
agreed to a TV. Happy nights

radiator warmth.   I liked those days before
backtalk   friends   hours on the phone

then she was
no longer my child.

She moved away
met the boy   I liked him

and the marriage   people I didn't know
all around us.   Bright colors   aura

of strangers' smiles   she hugged those people.
I returned to my life   piano   my songs

water aerobics   restaurant meals
the occasional flight   mostly visits

by phone 'til she came for me   flew me
in my red fox coat one rainy night

to a new home   to live where garden shrubs
needed trimming after church.   I clipped

up and down the street 'til they were perfect

and she brought me here   to fluorescent
lights   jewel-toned women in flowing robes

*more people I don't know   meals at a long
table I return to morning and night*

*sometimes the familiar scent   onions
and ground beef   Oh, I am home.*

Four Chambers Redacted

Four chambers, an unglamorous hub of plumbing and electricity, the valves and pipes, nerve endings to the central station. Am I nothing more than a utility pole for my heart?

Imagine the child who hears *when did this happen* and then from an alarmist mother the 5-year-old knows *you have a heart condition.*

Imagine a virus that has nowhere better to go than into the myocardium of a 19-year-old, otherwise a normal college co-ed who is sent to infirmary for three months to resent, deny, write and rail against

bedrest and lingering fever until one day she is sprung to a life of *you have a heart condition* which does not stop her from hours of tennis, a cigarette habit, late nights and love and along the way,

the old guy who says *I'm developing a machine that can see as well as hear your heart.* Fabulous as the echocardiogram has become was the loop of his body and shy eyelashes at the foot of the bed.

Words *murmer, mid-systolic click, acute viral myocarditis but the fever cleared,* tuned my ears to the whispers I heard at night, pressed against my pillow, *loosh-p-phoosh, loosh-p-phoosh*—friendly moments with my congenital flaw.

Chest pains and a career worthy of all of them, marriage, kids, EKGs and cardiologist exams, a growing familiarity with shortness of breath, a brush with congestive heart failure, a new drumbeat of *someday your valve will have to be replaced*, and the steady friendly whispers.

The sounds assured me of wins against my flaws by living every day, being 'normal' while holding back from the biggest hikes, finding excuses like not leaving children to avoid the highest peaks.

Imagine that from 5 to 45, *you have a heart condition* becomes a given, an anthem of dubious distinction, like buying groceries, changing diapers or managing careers. Something to attend to because if that goes away, life might slip with it.

Imagine that suddenly your heart is shattered, the figurative million pieces that fall away from your put-together core as kids turn into rebels and your one heart constant disintegrates. Your love has perished.

The million pieces of you fall in silence everywhere for a year and the whispers inside sound the only stable ground,

a path to the million futures you must piece back together for teenagers, expectant family and your own decision to remain alive.

Convertible

I can't tell you which American beauty it was—
top rolled back—
and it came with my brother in a pressed white T.
I'd barely met him but instantly saw
the almond eyes with dark bags
our father called valises.

This ended my visit with our father, his mother, our sister
at their brick house with its front and back porches
its elm trees, shaded cushioned chairs and the hammock
I occupied in my white, brown, and blue
polka dot bikini, sipping the Tom Collins
my father poured for me as I considered
family and the smell of mothballs and Pledge.

My brother in his fine Fruit of the Loom
burst into the house with cheerleader gusto,
gathered me into that car like a kid from school,
generous with smiles and good-guy swagger,
he loaded me in   luggage and linen suited   formal
for flight in the seventies   grinned sidelong at me
as he gunned across the Brooklyn Bridge.

He asked about my favorite subjects   *I like English*
Pulling at my collar   *poetry and fiction.*
I teach biology he said with a grin.
Kind of him to take me to the airport
—*no problem*—he might have said.
I really liked having a brother   that hour   that open car
a sibling   sudden as the summer breeze.

Behind the Moon

    —1969, Apollo 11

As war and protests against it
                      raged on earth,
                                        fire spit men into the skies

                      to walk on the moon.

My haze was being sixteen,
                    theirs the pitch

                            through atmosphere to space.

                      I conjured pinpricks of life in an infinite
surround.

My mother cried
                  as Houston and the world

                                    listened.

                  47 minutes.

                  Silence as they crossed the side no one could see.

My mother must have breathed.
                  I did

                            when astronaut voices
sounded from Houston.
                A big exhale.

47 minutes

                                    away from my mirror, the revolution against
Vietnam

black skin, city sweat, humans sparking,

                                                            shape-shifted.

Somehow

                            walking the lunar surface.

                            seemed easier than those.

The Face of the Moon

I carried my newborn in a front pack
pressed against my chest. She gazed at me
with wide, china blue eyes until
some combination of motion and contentment lulled her lids to a close
and her head listed into my waiting hand. I could feel her breath
if I put a finger close to her nose, and sometimes her puckered lips
reflexively sucked for a few seconds before relaxing into deeper sleep.
I looked at her with feelings no human can calculate or conceive
until becoming a parent for the first time, her pale fresh skin,
iridescence interrupted by the contours of almond shaped eyes
the lids themselves delicate in natural pastels, a round face
with supple checks, wisps of blonde hair, a shimmery hint of eyebrows,
and that Cupid-bow mouth.
Cupping her head in my hand, I breathed in,
imagining that I held the moon—
perfect, silent and suspended until the break of day.

Landing

The coat on the old lady who stepped off the plane,

all those foxes killed

                        in the name of style,

They bore down on my mother's tiny frame

as she doddered off our flight into

                        a California downpour.

I had rescued her from Chicago to be closer,

out of the danger posed

                        by a fleeting mind

and unyielding demands

like wearing her red fox

                        into the storm.

A Child Of The Fifties Looks Out On A Lake

The sand is imported here to make a beach
on the shores of this mountain lake, where families
pile in for fifties-style fun. Grills sizzle and send up
aromatic invitations to gather as scrawny boys tumble
into a dad's pickup bed, a squirming mass of scapulas,
lake-tousled hair, ribs articulated against white skin
under a generous sun, against the shimmering water.
Kayaks, canoes and large beach umbrellas shine
like baubles against the lodgepoles towering here,
serene background in a whispering breeze.
How like it has always been, I muse.

In the grip of this scene, I jolt. What happened?
Don't these people know?

That night another scene spools yet again.
I'm going to a store to get baby shoes, maybe
look at dresses. Like it used to be,
like it cannot be now because
of the danger, the panic I feel
if someone unmasked
gets too close. Urgent
steps back, impulse
to flee, stay away, stay away.

Under the blaze of the same sun
over a different lake in an earlier time
it was also true. What you cannot see lurks,
still like the thing that maimed long ago
in wait to sicken and kill—new, ghastly, now.
Don't they know?

Just Kids Again

Seems like Sinatra sang all night, like
we talked all night. I'm not sure who

was my date, who was with anyone, we were
just friends together in our last hours as kids.

We were obviously paired for the ritual dinner
and dancing, and after—the retreat poolside

atop a Gold Coast high rise where we knew
the rite of passage was to stay awake.

We sank into lounge chairs, a last conversation for some
before new worlds absorbed us, making this moment sweet.

Those songs bring back the boys—in suits as if men then,
before they "made it" and one succumbed—

simple tunes take me
to that shoreline,

orange out of darkness over an opaque lake.

Horsemen of Earlier Years

In my remembering of that time
cotton-haired folks pottered in high-ceilinged rooms
of urban mansions until they breathed no more, expired
without the drama of blinking screens or chemical remedy
—simply dropped one Tuesday or Saturday
having run the course of their upright years.

Even my father who seemed to die many times over
as his heart failed and failed again
fought back to life beyond all reasonable expectation
then finally went,
his last breath a soft-spoken last stand.

In those days of immortality
the teenaged boy whom I babysat when we were kids
crashed on the Outer Drive
one night as the moon hijacked the lake
and sand three lanes to the east.

Another gossamer boy ended it after high school
just as quietly as he had materialized
between classrooms and study halls.

I heard that our class valedictorian battled MS in the city I had left.
His distant death *quaedam probationem*, opening my eyes,

finally, to horses ready at my door.

You cry out,

*Words come
but I fall silent.*

*Now I know
to tune my ears.*

III

Seeker's Poem

To drive the fawn road
lined in xanthous bloom,
scotch broom
under lavender wisps;

to approach
the darkening sky
up a wild palette
to grey and white,

the rain, the sweet
scent of grass.
To breathe in,
to quiet.

*

To find wooden houses
once home to soldiers,
rimming a parade ground,
now clapboard portals,

host to ghosts who never go.
To learn a concrete bunker
stores sacred remains,
boards of a canoe.

*

Tribes lift their paddles
as they come to shore now
in carved vessels, seasoned
and salted by Juan de Fuca.

These are spirits we are told
don't touch our boats.
Don't disturb them
with your churning.

Young men rescue the old spirit
from the bunker,
shoulder the timbers
to a strait side fire.

Licking flames
lift the vessel.
Smoke
into crepuscule,

*

up, up above
the dreamy chorus
against still sand,
Olympic rise,

high over towns and passes
Siskiyou Smith Hill
Canyon Creek
and rivers

Willamette   Umpqua
Clackamas   Coquille
Malheur   to reunite
with stories no longer told.

Ghost Tree

Tamaracks on the lakefront,
craggy bark
mirrored, green
between earth and sky,
but for one
that breaks the line.

White, gnarled
branches
with sliver tips,
twisting to the summit

nearby where men scrabbled
laying railroad to the coast,
the whiteout pass
where travelers ate their own,
the rivers and streams
where seekers rushed for gold.

Did any of them make camp
beneath your once-lush canopy?
Old tree, what history
haunts the hollows of your core?

Blizzards howl and toss
live branches, snapping trees
like twigs in hellbent sway.
Snow banks bend and hobble
trunks to submission. Yet

you, white thing, stand
spectral and unspoken.

Stonehenge

Downward rays
break roiling clouds
Boulders rest in chalk
and grass overrun
with humanity in baggy pants,
rumpled in all colors,
striking poses for those
more interested in the camera
than what went on here
compelling ancients to haul
massive stones into formations
astronomical, physical and spiritual
circles destroyed and twice rebuilt
for reasons the stone haulers
now fully contained in nearby dirt
mounds with their secrets
knew well then
and now only over-photographed
except by one woman
in perimeter grass, long,
legs out-stretched, head tilted
as if listening,
sunglasses not hiding the gaze,
arms back bracing her,
ribs thrust open
watching.

I think she is breathing in
where winter solstice casts
its shadow in one precise line
and summer solstice shines
an opposite stance, the wisdom
of a calendar, the seasons
and the mystery
of those early people
hauling and building
this balance of rocks,

circle of stones on chalk,
on a ghostly foundation,
its outer circle
its grassy dent.

Day of the Deer

What do you want? Why are you here?

I said to the deer that lay in my lawn
a mottle of brown on grass like straw.
He gazed at me   I waited 'til answered
by a rustling breeze blowing golden
bay leaves from branches through trees,
flakes gusting the yard between the buck
and me. Then he rose   six points
to the sky   ambled uphill

into the trees   into the shade   away.

What do you want? Why are you here?

I say as a young deer rests at lawn's edge
two craggy horns angle   ears twitch and turn
to new sounds on the breeze.
Haze and pine dust
barely conceal six points behind him
the big blinking buck.

The two bring back another day   when we learned
our time would be short.   We knew when deer after deer
appeared   stood somber   stayed.

Wrong Turn

I didn't mean to turn   clearly   wrong
as if I'd never   again and again   every day those five months
into the stretch past construction   to the left
to the building   its valet parking

now my hybrid whispers by   memory   hush
harp strings reverberating from high ceilings
red pine floors pharmacy to waiting room
examining room to lab   to infusion   therapy for the willing
those who fight on   or fold   under the glare

our waiting is over now   your end came   there have been years
missed turns and turns waiting to be made   I'm here again
passing through on my way to life   as it is now
the road found me   still under so much construction

Clear despite my tears   flat pavers
high portico   sheltered passageway
the valets eyed my car   it was after hours
the treated sick had gone home

there is no one here for me   I don't need to be
the business of my life is close by   a campus
kids on bikes   crescent moon   hung in the electric sky.

Curator

A house empty of voices, silent after peals and calls,
simple now, a swordfish dinner at the family table
for one who studies storied walls.

Shadowboxed here, a Chinese temple artifact—nine beasts
embodied in a dragon with thunderbolt tail—its twisted
torso and gilt-leafed grin—chary and divine.

And there, antiquity in golden glow—
double-gabled bowers hold suitors to three maidens
in midair drift between lily pond, and bamboo culms.

Light-strokes trace coastal reveries decades before
the artist's dense-oil forests—hanging on a distant wall.
Penciled Ohio River flooding, marks the start

of palette shifts to dancing jungle primitives and farm
animals in bold blues and reds that cavort
with Miro above the baby grand across the room.

Flat walls and silence freeze rollick—hold these scenes
and the one who chose and set them making something new
—the once-complete now facets in a larger frame.

Seen in Stone

—Doug

I haven't seen him since.

Is he there in the night-time
behind a fence in shadow?

A lone dog howls
from a cavernous space
a mournful bass
piercing the dark.

       He doesn't step out to me,
       yet

in my mind's eye
shaggy dark hair, lean frame,
and the scent of fresh leaves,
the him of our early days

       steeped in shadow,
       in the night breeze.

Sirens weh-wah weh-wah
through Paris streets
as dark steels
to morning.

Through cell and sleep,
I feel him still.

Outside the shadows,
cathedral bells clang the day
I am present
meeting past in stone.

You Rode Your Horses

—For Michael

along the Humboldt coast
on seashell beaches,
river beds between redwoods.

Age-faded photos
frame a skinny man at home on a ranch
as he is in town now.

We're new together, you and I,
with lifetimes to learn about each other
and your Arabians

> *fifteen hands—quarter-horse size. Endurance animals
> from the desert, all others are from the Arab Barb.*

Sepia and static, the pictures freeze
their rocking gait, wide nostrils,
tails fanned and arched for the gallop.

Your animals of the seventies
named for constellations, idiosyncrasies,
the four winds, the occasional rock star

who restored you from city sadness, lifted you
to love their quirks and silent powers.
I see your smile about each one.

> *When I rubbed his butt, Obie would fart. I could run up behind
> Scoots, and jump on his back. Country Music was the champion.*

The seventies ticked away, you single,
touring, doing the music thing,
moving here n' there. You made it back.

> *They trust you when you're steady. They're social animals
> —only crazy when humans are.*

There your street-smart start gave way
to tongue clicks as you stroked medallion markings.

Dark eyes, orbital ears settled to your whisper.
You rode without saddle or bit.
I think horse sense steadied you through the decade—
ribbons, celebrity competitions, windfalls,
Black Monday.

> *Suddenly you couldn't give any of them away.*

Nothing changed for them that day, not the terrain,
the ranch, it's corrals, fences and troughs.
They pranced to pasture, accepted blankets for the chill,

stilled for grooming,
trotted back for nighttime meals.
You moved away again.

> *Solo in his stallion pasture, Country Music spent his last days*
> *with Doobie, the shepherd, and Asshole, the ram.*

You didn't get there,
having gone
where horses cannot go.

With you still, the salt breeze
that slapped your brow, their neighs,
nickers, blows and snorts,

the hay-barn smell,
the rutted trails you've ridden
to shores we call our own.

Slightly

What lives now
the Bormioli Rocco
glassware
that begs for an heir

to learn
the Negroni,
Bees Knees,
Italian Greyhound.

Drinks like dances
with words
to honor
those who have passed.

I knew you slightly
before the story
of tomato seeds
rolled into newsprint.

Another day
sports or headlines
equal contenders
to preserve the seed.

A grandfather's habit
passed to a son,
your father, then you
finding a stash after.

And now in the telling.
Their story lives.
You to me.
Tips about tomatoes.

The seeds are small, we are.
But we raise a glass and live
to know each other better
in our slight time.

Orb

You brought me
a small brass orb
at the center of nine

dark rings that circle
on a burnished stand
the axis that might

have swirled the globe
of our yesteryears
but here the solar system

newly turns around the sun
as music brings
morning and the day

awakens
flesh

settles grief
into light

the sun turns
and the planets stick
in their magnetic spin

lips meet,
in song and alchemy
with hydrogen and iron.

Photographer's Proclamation

There will be photos when this child
is born.

All of us will talk of fingers and toes
in a new language,

descended as we are, from ancient
empires and reserved Scandinavians.

We will marvel with the tired new parents.
at hair and eye colors never before known.

We will hover and I will photograph.
And then I will stop.

I want to hold my progeny, my daughter,
her man

without images
before the world begins.

Quaero

On this earth, little one,
we spin, and we turn as I do
with you in my arms,

your eyes tight shut,
your spring peach cheeks.
Little boy blue,

when our gaze moves
from you, quivers
and coos draw us back,

a gravity miracle
for a son
so small.

Yes, there's a meadow
of sheep, cows and corn
These rhymes among many,

I give from my heart
with stars and a horn
you may blow in the storm,

with archangels who circle
the blaze and rotations,
a sun that commands

your gaze. Awake now,
you turn from the glare
to rest in my eyes.

Hello Grief, Garden, Hawk

Tomorrows appear like apparitions. Dickensian ghosts
whisper a future taking shape every day.
Please tell me why sadness
holds me. By now we're dear friends.

The sun rises and sets. When is the day new?

I work to transform my Eden, not for perfection but production
of crops untouched except by my hands. Meanwhile my spirit
hawk shrieks, hunts, lurks and soars—there for me to imagine.

I, too, soar, yet the sunny skies—heavy, longing.

Time now hangs like a weight, a bucket to fill with all that is
precious. As if to an altar, I bring our forebears, our new babies,
hope for health and soft landings. New dawnings.

Sapphires, generations, brussels sprouts, high nests,

safe perch. The first real tomorrow with grief, garden, hawk,
I dream it, time with old friends finding our way.

Another Moment in the Garden of Eden

The mad surge of zucchini leaves over-take
artichokes, eggplants and cucumbers.
I cut them in a surgical removal all the while
hearing the hawk. He is frantic, a pulsing cry.
He circles overhead hunting, reminding me
of the hawk that dipped over my windshield
carrying a writhing snake. My back seizes
from the work, forcing me into the plastic
Adirondack chair.

It's so peaceful here. Tiny watermelons
form in a vine at my feet, a row of celery green
contrasts the blue of towering brussels sprouts.
This place is in formation with elevated boards
to support higher beds. Tonight I planted lettuce
starts as the sun slipped lower and leaves
perked up after a withering heat. Jays, crows,
towhees, certainly the leaf chewing finches
send their song into the canyon.

Today the hawk perched at the top of a tree,
defying a twig so small, perhaps not the girth
of his stocky legs, twigs gripped in talons.
What is it to be this god of the sky, insistent
in a soprano call, perched with smaller birds
flying at him, attacking in their own shrieks?
He complains immobile from his perch,
they shriek. The nest they protect, well,
this world is imperfect but the dominant

hawk, now bored, moves on, lifts with
no riffle to the tree-top, dips low as if
seeing me, as if I am too large, too tough,
not suited to survival the way he prefers
it. And I lift with him wondering at his loft
and toughness, talon strength, gentle landings.
He threatened the nest and the little birds
fought him off. They thought. Clever devil.
What is he hoping for today?

Notes

"Being. Father."
Inspired by Ian Brown's *The Boy In the Moon*.

"On Death Row"
Troy Anthony Davis was executed September 21, 2011 by lethal injection in a Georgia state prison at age 42 after a 22-year incarceration for the murder of a security guard at a Savanna Burger King. His trial included multiple witnesses who later recanted their stories. Though Sylvester "Redd" Coles was later implicated and allegedly confessed to the killing, multiple appeals, a Supreme Court-ordered evidentiary hearing and appeals by numerous human rights groups failed to overturn the execution.

"Meditation on Kinsukuroi"
Kintsugi, also known as *kinsukuroi*: the Japanese art of repairing broken pottery by mending the areas of breakage with lacquer dusted or mixed with powdered gold, silver, or platinum, a method similar to the maki-e technique. As a philosophy, it treats breakage and repair as part of the history of an object, rather than something to disguise.

"Silent No More"
Inspired by Ai Wei Wei's installation titled "Straight" in the Royal Academy of Arts, London 2017

"Of Men Who Stayed"
Inspired by a news story following the 2011 Fukushima earthquake and tsunami in Japan about fifty workers who stayed inside the leaking nuclear reactor. International media widely reported that they assumed that they had given up their lives in the effort to save others from the impact of the radiation.

"Imperfect Perfect"
Inspired by a conversation with a young woman who performed in numerous musical theater productions while growing up. At 29, she was completing her MEd, after several years teaching in the area. She has Cerebral Palsy and is wheelchair/screen bound. She is a smart, joyous and enthusiastic communicator.

Mary Pacifico Curtis is a Silicon Valley entrepreneur, seasoned branding and PR professional, and author of poetry and non-fiction. Published work includes her recent memoir, *Understanding Moonseed*, two poetry chapbooks, *Between Rooms* and *The White Tree Quartet* (WordTech's Turning Point imprint), and numerous pickups in literary magazines and anthologies.

Accolades include recognition as a 2012 Joy Harjo Poetry Finalist (Cutthroat Journal), 2019 Poetry Finalist in *The Tiferet Journal*, non-fiction finalist in The 48th New Millennium Writings contest and a 2021 non-fiction finalist in *The Tupelo* Quarterly Open.

At 24, she founded Pacifico, Inc., which grew into one of Silicon Valley's largest independently owned PR and branding firms with clients that included many global technology leaders. When both daughters went off to college, she earned an MFA in 2012 in creative writing at Goddard College.

Curtis lives with her husband in the foothills of the Santa Cruz mountains on a terraced property where she grows vegetables and fends off gophers while admiring deer, coyotes, wild turkeys and the occasional bobcat.

www.ingramcontent.com/pod-product-compliance
Lightning Source LLC
Chambersburg PA
CBHW031125160426
43192CB00008B/1118